BARREN HARVEST

Barren Harvest

Selected Poems

Dane Zajc

Translated from the Slovenian by
Erica Johnson Debeljak

White Pine Press • Buffalo, New York

Terra Incognita Series, Volume 8

Series Editor: Aleš Debeljak

WHITE PINE PRESS
P.O. Box 236, Buffalo, New York 14201

Publication of this book was made possible
by grants from the
Trubar Foundation;
the Slovenian Ministry of Culture;
the Slovenian Academy of Arts and Sciences;
the National Endowment for the Arts;
and with public funds from the
New York State Council on the Arts, a State Agency.

Cover photograph: Copyright © 2004 by Tomo Brejc

Book design: Elaine LaMattina

Printed and bound in the United States of America

First Edition

Library of Congress Control Number: 2003108959

CONTENTS

INTRODUCTION

THE BIOGRAPHY OF SOLITUDE
IN THE POETRY OF DANE ZAJC

Aleš Debeljak

IT WAS A PLEASANT MAY afternoon in the late nineties. Intimations of summer in Ljubljana, the capital city of Slovenia, were already visible. Fresh air languidly rose up from the slow-flowing green river and enveloped the old city quarter under the medieval castle in the promise of things to come. The improvised gardens in front of the restaurants had emerged only days before. Sun rays revived memories of the bygone bourgeois time, locked in the cobble-stoned streets that had been laid out during the long reign of the Viennese royal House of Hapsburg, the dynasty that ruled the Slovenian lands until its empire disintegrated at the end of World War I. Slovenia and its people, however, have persisted in this patch of Europe wedged between the Alps and the Mediterranean, between the Balkan moiuntains and the vast Hungarian plains.

Dane Zajc and I sat at the table in front of a popular café, "Nostalgia," sipping capuccino and enjoying long silences in our meandering conversation. The glaring sun of summer was not yet the order of the day. No need, then, for sunglasses. They remained in their cases on the table. Dane's restless hands, speckled with the brown spots of a man in his early seventies, would come to rest on the surface of the table, from time to time toying with the case. Then they would just as suddenly retreat to a pyramid of his long fingers. Dane Zajc is the greatest living Slovenian poet, not only according to professional opinion but also according to the general popular consensus, a combination that is extremely difficult to attain in matters of literature. I daresay, alas, that the pedestrians passing by did not know who he was. If an artist today wants to reach an audience wider than interpreters of useless words, humanities students, and other poets, he must subjugate his creative neuroses to the demands of the consumer market. He must transform his words into a conveniently formulaic wisdom that can be compressed into a happy soundbite, with which Eastern European countries have, for better and worse, become increasingly familiar since the "velvet revolution" of 1989 and the fall of the Berlin Wall.

Dane Zajc, however, was born in 1929, too early for this particular form of subjugation. He spent the first fourteen years of his life in a remote village in the Slovenian mountains. During the Second World War, German occupying soldiers burnt his family home to the ground. As a sometime courier for the Partisan resistance, Zajc occasionally descended to the valley, but he spent most of his time working a miserable plot of a vegetable garden to help his family survive—a family that lost its two elder sons to the war. The intimate world of the young poet was thoroughly defined by the experiences of nature and violence. It might have been an education of sorts, but it was certainly not a sentimental one.

His work, on the other hand, was not divorced from sentimental influences, though Zajc was able to fend off a stifling dependence on his early inspiration. In addition to Slovenian writers, the formative sources of Zajc's poetic work were Russians, Russians, Russians. No wonder: Slovenia was, until 1991 when it attained full independence, part of Yugoslavia, a patchwork of diverse peoples, cultures, languages, and religions that its unchallenged leader, Marshal Tito, controlled with the cunning mind of a grand diplomat and the iron hand of a communist despot. The eastward-looking orientation of Tito's imperium left a deep mark on generations of writers who were not only isolated from democracy and capitalism but also from Anglo-American aesthetics. In their youth, the generation that Dane Zajc belongs to, learned instead the poems of Jesenin and Pushkin by heart. Lermontov and his stormy romantic exaltation, his disarming pessimism, his rapturous sensuality: all of these aesthetic forces shot into Zajc like bolts of lightning during the decade spanning the late forties and early fifties. In the work of Salzburg pharmacist George Trakl and in the urban elegies of Baudelaire's *Les Fleurs du Mal,* Zajc later discovered the strange and beautiful horror that made his lifelong association with the voiceless people possible.

"There was only enough room left for Anna Akhmatova and the uncompromising poetry of witness," said Zajc, taking a long drag on his Marlboro Light. He discovered the ingenious Vladimir Hlebnikov, the multiple melancholic mirrors of Andrej Tarkovsky, the documentary sharpness of Italian neo-realists, the carnal knowledge of Federico Fellini, and the repressed passion in the films of Ingmar Bergman. The roster is, I suppose, fairly predictable. Dane Zajc, after all, came of age in the era when Stetson hats and silk stockings, Montgomery raincoats and cigarette lighters—precious goods on the black market of consumer items that the Communist party deemed unsuitable—were smuggled in from Italy. It was somewhat easier to breathe in the cultural sphere. Ljubljana art houses rolled not only weekly propaganda reels but also serious artistic films by contemporary Western and Eastern European directors. Thus the Communist party catered to the appetites of the masses hungry for novelty and widened the horizons of youthful audiences, who were not fed a diet of mass-produced American dreams as they are today.

Now, after the fall of the Berlin Wall and the end of the Cold War, we love and hate, it seems, under a canopy of illusion about democracy and the freedom of "the end of history." In this context, we don't even mockingly laugh any more at socialist realism because its pedagogy of working class heroism has become so hopelessly passé. At the same time, we seem to be closing our eyes to the waves of aggressive advertising and its sublime aesthetic of an organic harmony and attractive shape, the signature component of capitalist realism. This is perhaps even more pernicious than socialist realism, its outdated counterpart, which up through the 1960s was the enforced aesthetic orthodoxy in Eastern Europe. Capitalist realism is arguably more pernicious, for it insinuates itself into the minds of consumers as it beguiles them, with increasing success, into replacing any meditation on the beautiful and the good with the enjoyment of beautiful consumer goods. In the process it commodifies not only the products themselves but the mental frame within which the enjoyment of them takes place. The most this illusion can do is provide a formal fascination, which can no longer be compelling on an existential level. Today, if you want to retreat from the unceasing flow of images, music and words to the temporary haven of art, you must voluntarily isolate yourself to find time for contemplation, perhaps even for the grace of epiphany.

In the political sphere, Yugoslav communists did not experience an epiphany. It was, rather, pragmatism that made them recognize the need for the relative independence of the artistic imagination in the wake of the self-preserving break with Stalin in 1948. Consequently, they revoked the so-called theory of the "Partisan birch tree," which demanded that an artist include in each and every artwork a reference to the ideological narrative of the proletarian revolution. Even such an innocuous artistic genre as landscape painting had to contain a birch tree under which a Partisan figher could rest, thus revealing the artist's commitment to the red horizons of communist utopia. The authorities explicitly recognized aesthetic autonomy at the Yugoslav Party Congress in 1958, though they have applied it in an admittedly selective manner. That was the year that Dane Zajc finally succeeded in publishing his first book of poetry, *Burnt Grass,* although the printing was undertaken at his own expense. The book, while not officially banned, was next to impossible to obtain on the market.

Dane Zajc had no desire to close his eyes to the fruits of totalitarianism's barren harvest. In his book, he confirmed the primacy of the individual over the collective and summoned a sense of human mortality in order to combat the Potemkin villages of communism. Not only in aesthetic terms, but also in terms of moral opposition, Dane Zajc was engaged in the struggle against the dictates of the regime. Zajc's growing distance from the Yugoslav government of "workers, farmers and honest intellectuals" was tangibly spelled out in 1951, when Zajc spent three months in jail. Zajc had performed at a public literary reading. A zelous informant reported his alleged anti-regime pronouncements and Zajc, branded a "verbal delinquent," was sentenced to one month of solitary confinement before being transfered to the common prison. At that time, Zajc's political stigma should have earned him a trip to the Naked Island, Tito's transplantation of a Stalinist gulag to a rocky island in the Adriatic Sea.

Zajc's mother, a simple peasant, had long maintained a stoic silence, but when Zajc was imprisoned, she walked to the head-quarters of the political police in the center of Ljubljana and somehow found her way to those in charge. "She banged her fist on the table and exclaimed, 'I've given you two sons, I won't give you a third,'" Zajc told me, and took another sip from his cold capuccino. I offered him another cigarette and for a while we silently watched the schoolgirls and the rare tourists making their way past our table at the café. Zajc was ultimately not sent off to the labor camp, but he was thrown out of high-school and sent to the military service, where he spent two long years in the olive green uniform of the people's army.

After he got out, Dane Zajc helped to found an important cultural journal, *Revija 57*. An explosive and provocative periodical that introduced existentialism into the Slovenian public sphere, it didn't last long. However, even after 1964, when the communist authorities banned yet another dissident magazine, *Perspektive*, Dane Zajc did not relent, though he had to wait until the death of Tito in 1980, when volatile political conditions were sufficiently relaxed to allow for the monthly publication, *New Review,* which Dane Zajc helped establish. It was a forum for the intellectual nationalism which played a decisive role in creating the foundation for an independent Slovenian state. At the end of the eighties, Zajc recognized the increased relevance of civil disobedience, having participated in the oppositional Commission for Human Rights, in numerous demonstrations and at protest readings at the Association of Slovenian Writers; events designed to radically challenge communism's grip on power.

Shadows over our "Nostalgia" table grew longer. The air turned more chill, and Zajc grew silent again. While his habit of silence may be annoying for the interviewer, it is an inspiration for the reveller. Alone in my thoughts, I thus conjured a particularly poignant image. I pulled it from the archive of my personal memory. What did I see? I saw the dimmed hall of France Prešeren Club in the Ljubljana neighborhood of Trnovo. The alternative theater appears, despite the addition of new velvet curtains, as what it once was: a forum for amateurs. Hovering above the squeaky wooden chairs of the front row, I see the faces of excited poets who have gathered to see the greatest of the great in our literary profession. Photographers crouch before the low stage. In the jam-packed hall, an audience of more than one-hundred and fifty sip beer, smoke and wait patiently. It is April 1994 and finally evenings of live poetry have resumed at the Club. To describe this particular performance, the Slovenian language is most appropriate with its denial of a distinction between a song (that comes from a throat) and a poem (that lies written on a blank page). In English, there is a barrier between the two notions; in Slovenian, it is the same word. *Dane Zajc and Janez Škof: Recital for Poetic Words and Accordion.* Two bodies, one world, a broken barrier. In the magical circle that the two performers invisibly drew in the air of the theater hall, a recognition of pain was slowly born.

The poetic works of Dane Zajc emerged as the symbol of a wound, a wound inflicted by man's indebtedness to his own death. What is repressed in the human being as a mortal creature, returns in the language of the human being as a lethal creature.

As Zajc shudderingly reveals in the poem "Barren Harvest," violence is the primordial truth of the world. Zajc's poetic description of the horror of his brother's death is one of the political reasons why he could not bring out his first collection with an official publishing house. That the revolution, in the name of which communists justified the death of so many fallen partisan fighters and civilians, might indeed prove to be but a compromised barren harvest, unworthy of immense suffering was simply not a tenable conclusion to the arrogant all-powerful authorities. Here, then, is a part of his poem, which has entered public vocabulary in Zajc's home country:

> *I recognize his skull, mother said,*
> *by its beautiful white teeth.*

Beautiful white teeth
biting into the soil,
beautiful brown eyes
filled with soil,
strong white bones
that once were hands,
hands that never carressed a woman,
strong youngs bones
carressing the soil.

...

Inconceivable is the harvest
of beautiful brown eyes,
the barren harvest
of the unfeeling earth.

In his second collection, *Tongue of Soil*, published in 1961, Dane Zajc rejected both the political and the aesthetic assumptions of the day. He created a new language, a new tongue, a tongue of soil that speaks words of clay. This innovative concentration on the earth's most material aspect lent him a certain relaxation and warmth, yet at the same time demonstrated the power of destruction, revealed as fire in the mouth. In order to create, the poet—the eternal outsider—had to conquer his fear of discovery. Zajc knew that black crows will kill a white one. Moreover, he knew that this was not merely a characteristic of the then communist cultural and political hegemony, but also and above all, a description of the primordial mythical narrative of any collective in any historical epoch. In his search for a new language, Dane Zajc often approached, and even transgressed, the border that divided poetry from mysticism. The mystic feels that words are not sufficient and for this reason he grows silent. The poet, for the same reason, sings on. The poet must always try to gather the elemental words from a life which lacks mythical totality. He must gather meaning from the cawing of crows above solitary mountains, from the the movement of things in a morning breeze, from strangers, from children, from the same, in another world, the same. To absorb the ritual incantation in the poems of Dane Zajc implies a surrender to another world, a world of magical enchantment and sacrifice, to Biblical parallelism and to the authority the ancient Greek choruses used to command.

It is not merely a biographical detail to note that for nearly a quarter of a century Dane Zajc has been the fortunate renter of a cottage in the highlands above the glacial Bohinj Lake. Zajc is a passionate moutaineer who is not intimidated even by dangerous winter expeditions. In his attachment to the Alpine world of rugged peaks and abandoned high mountain pastures, in his attachment to the world of sharp edges, it is necessary to recognize the fundamental source of Zajc's poetic vocabulary. Birds, ravines, insects, blindingly bright light, vipers, sky, water and mountains are at home in his vision: all of these are signs of the eternal continuity of being.

Another recollection, another image: one autumn day in 1990 —or perhaps it was spring—I met Dane in the United States. This was the first time we had met there. At that time, American readers did not have access to even a single anthology of Slovenian writers and English translations of Slovenian poetry books could be counted on a carpenter's hand (that is to say, a hand with three fingers missing). Dane and I had come from an anonymous national tradition to perform in a culture where the yoke of anonymity is carried only by individuals. Dane's young readers saw him as a great poet, regardless of his reputation in Slovenia, about which, in any case, they knew nothing. Deep individual immersion in his poetry demonstrated that good art knows no temporal limits, ethnic prejudices or international opinion. In spite of the necessary awkwardness caused by linguistic borders, which are the borders of the world, a good poem, even through the veil of translation, will plant a kiss on the most intimate part of its reader because to be good, it must speak of an archetypal situation in which the reader discovers with astonishment her own portrait. Precisely because of this quality, Zajc's grateful American readers invited him to lead a three-day workshop in Chattanooga, Tennessee—the kind of workshop with which the self-involved country between the Atlantic and Pacific oceans teems. I was completing my doctoral dissertation at a university in New York at the time, so I was already familiar with the institutionalization of poetry as a discipline. Poetry is taught at colleges in such a way that participating writers acquire not only craft and skill but also a nomadic micro-collective which in the enormous spaciousness of this disturbing and fascinating culture cannot hope for the advantages of European café society and other more spontaneous forms of social life. Here I will leave aside the thought that the café, like most traditionally civilizing institutions in contemporary Europe, is disappearing into the fog of nostalgic myth. I will instead offer what I hope is a revealing anecdote from this meeting.

For several hours, Zajc had been sitting motionless on a worn, green armchair in the living room of Richard Jackson, a poet and literature professor who had written about Zajc in a number of lucid essays. The party unfolding around him was reaching a crescendo of sorts. There was not a quiet corner in the house. Of course, it was only appropriate to have a celebration at the end of the workshop and the lectures on the use of style in contemporary poetry. Dane Zajc probably didn't much care about style. Why would he? He had only ever mastered one style: his own. The one that emerged from the aching marrow in his bones. If a man writes a founding tablet in the spiritual architecture of his people, the lush ornamentation in the new confessionalism or the experiments of the new formalism may justifiably fail to interest him greatly, if at all. Central to his interest is the way his own dark obsessions can be expressed in a poem that is as fragile as it is lyrical. There he sat: the greatest living Slovenian poet in a hospitable house in the middle of suburban nowhere, surrounded by a throng of gifted honors students and ignorant daddy's girls, frustrated editors of literary supplements, and romantic college bards. Zajc gazed into the crowd of stoned, enervated and eroticized students, as well as at the American and European poets who had come to perform in the deep American South. Only the day before, all us had listened to Zajc's public reading with astonished respect. The audience was treated to a reading from a limited-edition booklet of poems: Michael Biggins' and Michael Scamell's translation of Dane Zajc's *Ashes,* in the series entitled "Poetry Miscellany Yugoslav Chapbooks" that was published by the creative writing program at the University of Tennessee. Dane Zajc didn't care much for all this attention. He felt the same indifference in 1982 when he was a visiting Fulbright writer at Columbia University in New York and Josip Brodsky, a Nobel Laureate, publicly described his work as "the great poetry of a small nation." The praise that Brodsky gave Zajc was definitely no small compliment. All the same, I believe that Zajc intuitively felt that praise, although alluring and desired, has a significance that belongs to the external order of things.

Of course, compliments, congratulations, awards and appreciative essays take on a certain importance in social terms. In terms of the existential impulse of art—which can touch a wounded soul because it emerges from a wounded soul—all of this carnival is of slight relevance. At the party in that Tennessee suburb, Dane Zajc rose from his chair only once. He approached a young woman who I, though I had attentively prowled the room, did not remember. The hero of Slovenian letters exchanged a few words with her. Even today, I recall the metaphysical shudder that overcame me when he responded to my provocation: "Hey, Dane! Go for it! It's your turn now!" With this exclamation, I attempted to celebrate the fact that grateful groupies do not belong only in the domain of pop stars and football players. But Zajc's response floored me. With a gentle voice, he whispered, "Solitude departed for an instant."

Barren Harvest: Selected Poems of Dane Zajc presented here for the first time in a comprehensive English translation, make solitude depart for an instant, offering the reader a glimpse into a world that is as ancient as it is modern. Poetry that springs from an understanding of solitude as the main feature of the human condition reminds us that we may transcend solitude only for an instant: even in the climax of erotic union between two bodies, orgasms are, in fact, two, not one. Poetry as a form of erotic consumation of the bond between humans is thus wedded to an impossible pursuit of totality and perfection. In this regard, the poetry of Dane Zajc calls out the deepest secret of existence, which is perhaps the only thing we truly share.

Barren Harvest

from
BURNT GRASS
1958

Dead Things

Rain laps at the stones.
Water stands in the hearth.
Rain wears away the oven.
Sand fills the cellar.

The vines grow wild.
The well crumbles.
The last wall collapses.

Thistles grow in the corner,
where the table once stood.
Quiet evening conversation,
father's elbow on the table.
Dead father.

Your elbow has decayed.
Your hand is soil.

Who will tame the vines.
Who will light the fire.
Who will dig up from beneath the hearth
the decaying faces of dead years.

Barren Harvest

I recognize his skull, mother said,
by its beautiful white teeth.

Beautiful white teeth
biting into the soil,
beautiful brown eyes
filled with soil,
strong young bones
that once were hands,
hands that never caressed a woman,
strong young bones
caressing the soil.

Full of brilliant young teeth
sown in the earth.

Each spring the earth blossoms.
The cruel hard earth
that swallows us in her dark jaws.
The death of old men is hard.
But harder still is the harvest
of beautiful brown eyes
eyes that have never seen a naked woman,
that have never been kissed by her
whispering lips: I'm yours
(eyes that have seen nothing yet).
Inconceivable is the harvest
of beautiful brown eyes,
the barren harvest
of the unfeeling earth.

I remember you, brother.
Our mother recognized
your white teeth.
Your young white teeth
were the earth's barren harvest.

To Be a Drop of Rain

To be a drop of rain on your breasts,
to be a bright clean drop of rain
on your thirsty skin,
to be a drop of restless rain
on feverish breasts,
to be a drop of rain absorbed by your body.

To be the kindling in your fire,
to be a flame in your fire,
to be a great flame
in the fire of your life,
to burn, to burn, to burn out
and become the ashes scattered
by the breath of your passion,
to feel nothing more, to want nothing more.

Only in annihilation is there peace and love,
only in annihilation is there endless loyalty,
dead things love with the peace of eternity,
oh to be a rock in the field
of your love.

Bells of a New Day

Wind. And rocks.
And cold.

Cold in the red sky.
Cold in the bluish peaks.
In the frozen moss.
Cold in the crimson blossoms.

Cold in the abyss,
where the fog spins
a ball of rancour,
a ball of nausea,
a ball of hysterical laughter.

The soft bells of the herd
herald the morning
high on the ridge.
The rocky shoulders of the mountains
emerge from dark waters.
Grim and immobile.
The wind rips by them,
an invisible sailboat.

Clouds, washing their cruel greedy hands
in the bloody lake of early dawn,
herald the morning.
The sky is blanketed in
a dance of bears.
Blanketed in a dark menace.

Cold settles on the earth.
The first light lies
dismembered on the rocks.
Fog simmers in the cauldron of the abyss.

You are alone in this world.
Like a rock is alone
and the wind sighs
past the mountain's craggy face.
With only this to comfort them,
the broken bells of the herd
ring in the new day.

The Captive Wolf

Run, run, run.
With velvet steps.
With sinewy wild legs.
Run quietly like a silent grey spirit,
run round your cage,
on the rotting leaves.

Run ahead.
Run back.
With open muzzle.
With red tongue.
Run like a grey shadow,
a grey silent shadow of hatred,
a grey shadow of contempt
in your cage.

Run. Run. Run.
Howl, howl
wild and cruel.
Where do packs of wolves run free?
Where do droves of grey spirits
float in the milky moonlight
at the center of an evil flock?
Where are the soft throats of sheep?
O gorge on the sweet blood of sheep.
O howl. Howl.

Why do you howl, wolf,
as the earth howls
when it is crushed by a mountain of rocks?

Why do you howl, wolf?
Why do you howl,
as if you had long black thorns
caught in your throat?

Vipers

On some abandoned shore,
where sand and wind speak
of eternity,

vipers crawl
beneath the rocks,
cold and dreadful,
they creep upon my heart.

I said to the vipers,
hungry for warmth:
Drink my blood.
Since what is blood for,
what is a river of desire for,
if it cannot flow,
if it is choked by the dam of reason.

Devour my heart.
My heart is too full for me.
Too full for me,
when it melts into the ice,
just as weeping stars melt
into the river.

Devour my heart.
And twist yourselves into a cold coil
in the cavity of my chest,
so that I can no longer watch
how the stars weep
from darkened lakes,
and how they yearn for the bright footsteps
left behind
in the blue velvet sky.

Devour my heart
and drink my hot blood,
cold dreadful vipers.

Everything is permitted
on this desolate shore
where sand and wind speak
of eternity,
only your heart must be torn out
and tossed into the vipers' hungry jaws.

from
TONGUE OF SOIL
1961

Lump of Ashes

For a long time you carried fire in your mouth.
For a long time you hid it there.
Behind a bony fence of teeth.
Pressed within the white magic circle of your lips.

You know that no one must catch scent
of the smoke in your mouth.
You remember that black crows will kill a white one.
So you lock your mouth.
And hide the key.

But then you feel a word in your mouth.
It echoes in the cavern of your head.

You begin to search for the key to your mouth.
You search for a long time.
When you find it, you unlock the lichen from your lips.
You unlock the rust from your teeth.
Then you search for your tongue.
But it isn't there.
You want to utter a word.
But your mouth is full of ashes.

And instead of a word
a lump of ashes rolls down
your blackened throat.
So you throw away the rusty key.

And you make a new language from the soil.
A tongue that speaks with words of clay.

Gothic Windows

1.

Don't speak to me.
Still your forked tongue.

Don't look at me.
I don't like your eyes.
Other eyes are watching me.
Still as broken gothic windows.

The sun shattered them.
The arrogant sun.
Shattered them
with a thousand rifles.

The stars sliced them
during the long deaf nights
with slender rapiers.
Sharp bright blades danced
before great unmoving eyes.
The face of the moon opened:
like a floodlit cavern,
her mouth gaped wide,
filled with laughter's massive stones.

And saintly women died,
their long translucent faces
drooping like the wounded wings
of white angels.

And the narrow shining eyes of the world closed.
A cool light death
on the blade of a star beam.
The drunken laughter of the moon
tumbled into the emptiness.

Don't look at me.
Other eyes are staring at me.
Narrow. Empty. Dead.
Sad.

2.

Come evening, rubies glow
upon your breast, Magdalena.
Two red rubies under a grey veil.
In the dusk of the cathedral.
In the white smoke of a snuffed candle.
Lift your veil.

Lift it: the dry rustling of sin
amidst the scent of prayer.
The stars will fall from your head
with a dry crackling sound.
The stars will run in a glistening stream
from your eyes into my open mouth.
The rubies from your body
will fall into my lap.
The moon will lick your flanks
with the red tongue of desire.

Lift your veil, Magdalena.
Tomorrow you will stand in a sprinkling of sunlight,
naked. Humiliated.
Mine.

3.

White hands on the sky.
White feet on the stones.
White saints in high windows.
Saintly women bathed in red light.
A body wrapped in red tulle.

I am a marble angel.
An angel without faith.
White feet.
White hands.
A body wrapped in grey canvas.
An angel who loves saints.

The saints undress in the windows.
The sun shines through their backs.
Yellow. Red.
Slowly the saints undress.
Their bodies evaporate into smoke.
Only the hands remain.
Only the feet remain.
A sign in the blue sky.
Solitude in the white stones.
A black cross disintegrating
in the old eyes of the cathedral.

4.

Where is the moonlight of your hair, saintly woman?
Who singed your head?
Your body burns in a fire.
Ashes rise from your body
beneath the sky's cold eyes.

The morning brought you upon its hands
like a ripened fruit.
The wind cauterized you
with a look. With its mouth.
A snake, sucking you up.

Your body is coiled like a withered vine.
You stare, a mouldering wooden candelabrum,
into the sky's wounding light.
Without the benediction of peace.

Ashes rise from your body.
Helpless.

I burn beneath the eyes of the sky.
A juniper bush.
The fiery soles of burning feet
dance on my body.
The ashes of the cremated fall into my mouth.
I am thirsty.

5.

Black devils,
devils with cats' eyes
torment the virgin.

We will pinch your breasts
with red hot forceps
for all your thoughts
for all your passions
for all your dreams in the long nights.

We will anoint
your virginal skin with fire.
(Where is my angel,
where is my angel, red carnation,
in the sky,
or on earth?)

Into your mouth,
your sinful mouth
we will pour liquid fire
that will burn like the kisses of a thousand fiends.
(Where is the night
that brought you
on vespers stars,
cold star between my loins?)
We will hang you by your hair
from the sickle of the moon.
We will pull every thought,
every sinful thought
from your brain with long needles.
(Where is my angel,

where is my devil,
in the stars
or in the cold tongue of the wind
on my belly?)

Mad devils,
black devils torment the virgin.

Far off in a field, the sun sows golden seeds of wheat
with its roughened hands.
Silence glimmers in afternoon's web.

6.

They held his head with forceps.

Your damned hearth.
Your damned bed where you conceive
your damned progeny.

We will chase you round the world.
Disgust will guide your steps.

We will scatter a swarm of scorpions
in the bed of your soul.
We will hang a hive of hissing wasps
in the cellar of your chest.
We will make a nest of squirming weasels
in your head.
Your happiness will be dead,
your eyes, a grave.

They put his memory upon a lance.
They twisted his heart upon a spit.

(Three crows killed a dove
in the blue window of morning.
The spiders spun a web of silence.
Man is nowhere.)

7.

The gods are falling.
Lightning snaps in their eyes.
The great circle of the earth rolls
from their hands.
The gods are falling. Exhausted.

Your soul smoulders in eternal fire.
Your blasphemous tongue
pierced with burning needles.
Stinking goats will mock you.

I run.
My mouth is filled with curses.
There's a huge voice in my mouth.
The gods have fallen.
The gods are falling.
Omnipotent. Adored.

I run.
A huge voice falls upon me.
Stones from my mouth
are driven from the sky
and fall upon my darkness.
I run to a great dancing void.
Drunk. Free.

Your body will be torn apart.
Ants will pick at your bones.
You will be naked and humiliated.

A great god will watch you.
Great and cruel.

8.

I struggle against myself.
Hand tearing at hand.
Leg entangled with leg.
Voice raised against voice.
Voice swallowing voice.

One eye to the east.
The other to the west.
Two ears devoured,
each on its own end of the world.

He who triumphs struggles
only against himself.
A flock of thoughts attacks.
Eternal. Persistent.
Pulled into the vortex.
And dashed to pieces.

His hands will rise up.
His finger will rise up.
A thousand parts of him will rise up.
We are not vanquished, his fingers will cry out.
We want battle, roars the grass
growing from his hair.
It will grasp.
It will struggle.

I lost my mouth.
I lost the house of my voice.

Nobody wins.

Dead Pines

We were shrunken with fear.
We were roots grabbing at the earth.
And it came, the anxious face of night.

The mountain's brow crushed us.
Buried us under stones.
Flogged us with voices.

Our skin fell away.
Our bones were tossed together.
Our roots grabbed for air.

Our bodies, thrashed by the sun,
twisted with desire:
To have green needles.
A leafy green crown.

In death, our image was severe.
It told its story, bony and gray:
Death is the blow.
Death is the maelstrom of the body.
A struggle beneath the still waters of darkness.

Cover your eyes.
Close the doors of hearing
before our silence.

Eyes

Forgotten faces come back to you.
Words come back.
The ones you cast off on the road.
They come back, the dim murmur from a muddy river.

You fear them.
You draw her eyes on the wall of darkness.
Wide as the gates of morning above the mountain.
You draw them with your finger,
hollow and watery.

You fear night's treachery.
You hear it creeping beneath your window
with the footsteps of a cat.
I have her eyes, you say,
drawn upon the wall of darkness.
I have her eyes,
her solitude and peace,
your charred soul whispers.
And in fear you shriek: *I have love.*

Bulls rush across your mouth.
A hand rises up from the murmur of words
cast off on the road and wipes out her eyes.

And you are defeated.
And your mouth is crushed
like grass on the road after the herd has passed.

from
CHILDREN OF THE RIVER
1962

CHILDREN OF THE RIVER

Hours

How lonesome are the midnight hours
as they incline their dark faces
above the quiet night fields.
How sad their bronzy throats
as they sing their song, coated in half-black silver.
The cupboards of their chests are empty.
Only the dark sounds of night have wandered in.
Their mouths are empty.
Empty and hungry.
How lonesome are the midnight hours.

Stranger

You left us long ago, Stranger.
For a long time you stood in a stony hollow,
quiet as a forgotten statue
and in the evening black flowers grew from the whiteness
        of your brow.
When spiders began to spin you into powdery webs
you emerged from your solitude.
You pulled the black flowers from your brow
and placed them quietly in her arms.

You were silent. You were drunk from the flowers.
Flowers which were believed to be white statuary
from the dusky paths of your thoughts.
Then you looked into her face.
Long, long you looked.
What did you see there, Stranger?
Did you hear what your flowers said
as they lay there in the dust?

You left us long ago, Stranger.
For a long time you fled along narrow tracks
and then every evening we would watch your dark shadow
as it lit a cold fire in the field.

The blue voices of cuckoos fade in a heavy beech grove.
A long stream of red sunset trickles from evening's mouth.
Night arrives from the other side of the world
with the face of a mysterious animal.
Night flees past you on the white legs of solitude.
The hours break, with their black hands, the shooting
        stars in the sky.
You are the moon on my pillow,
with a red flame you write on night's face.

One evening you set your shadow ablaze.
Brow. Hands. Legs.
Your chest.
Are you warm now, Stranger?
Was your cold spirit finally warmed
by the fire in your body?
You left us long ago, Stranger.
It's been a long time since you've been on any earthly field.

You burnt in the field.
The dark blossoms sputtered on your brow.
The wind scattered your cold fire.
And when the grey day rose above eastern caverns,
we knew that rain was falling in the empty shell
       of your brow.

Brown Call

The white legs of day come with quiet footsteps.
They come and they awaken things.
So that things will open their sleeping eyes.
So that they will open them and seek
what they lost in sleep.
Each thing will seek its sister.
So that things will be united with the sunlight.
So that nothing will be lost.
Nothing alone.
Nothing left out.

Open the lake of your eyes for me,
so that I may look into your sky,
at your white birds,
so that I may listen to the brown call of your eyes.

The call which you awaken.
The call which you call
and whose echo blossoms on my lips.

And my mouth is filled with the sweet scent of flowers.
The light is brighter than their fire.
Noon is higher and day is eternal
because you wander in its temple.

You give flowers their scent.
Into their hands you pour white rounded movements.
With your warm fire you ignite a bonfire of words
and in the morning the light of your love lies upon my hair.

Upon the hair with which you cover me every night,
so that I sleep as if I were sleeping in your body,
so that I no longer exist,
so that there's only you.

Only you will walk in the blue temple of day.
The light shining through your body
will run though my body and through my bones.
And I will no longer exist.
And there will be only you.
Because you are the tongue in my mouth.

You'll pay for everything.
You'll pay most for your birth.
A swarm of jeering birds will follow you
through life.
They will land on your chest
at your hour of peace
and your hour of anxiety.
Claims will be made.
And you will give and give.
But redemption will never come.
For nowhere is there forgiveness.
Nowhere is there redemption for man.
There is no value inside of you
with which you can pay.
You alone are the payment.

Who will light your path through the night.
When you go through the marshes, toward what light
        will you turn your eyes.
When you hang in the void, to whom will you call.
When you have no pillow, where will you lay your head.
The night is full of sounds, but how will you recognize
        the right one.
The night is full of lights, but which light is the light
        of your eyes.
Who casts the hook for night waters into your mouth.
Who follows you on your path.
Which teeth, white and foamy from loneliness and
        hunger, sink into your flesh.
Who will light a glimmer of hope when you die.
Who will wait for you at the crossroads at midnight.
Who will divert the two paths with ruthless hands.
Who will cut the ties.
What a sharp invisible knife.

The moments of your life shatter
like drops of water on a marble slab.
Will you now put together the shattered drop?
The sand will drink it.
The flower will wet its face with it.
The yellow butterfly will carry it upon its wings.
Who will put together the shattered drop?
In pain, you reach with waxen hands toward
   the butterfly.
The distance drinks it.
The sky swallows it.
You bend your head down and your head is sand,
it is a flower in the meadow,
a larch in the mountains.
The drops fall from the branches
and shatter on the rocks.
The flowers drink them.
The yellow butterflies carry them away.
Where is the beginning and end of things?
The whip of fate pursues us.
But who knows,
aren't we ourselves the whip and the back
and the hand that lets fall the whip.

from
SNAKE KILLERS
1968

Rain

The cadavers of memory grow quickly in the night
as rain falls upon the barren patches of their graves.
But your past doesn't help you in the least.
And the rats that abandoned your ship
proved long ago that you are already sinking.
Surely and inevitably.

Rain exists for itself. It doesn't fall through your
          thoughts because of you.
Locomotives pass through you during the long nights.
They beckon to your memory, pulling it into the wide
          expanses that you don't like to visit.
Perhaps you will withdraw into a slumber quilted with
          rain.
It doesn't really matter:
You awaken in the morning before a mountain of refuse
that you must crawl over:
because you want to see the meaningless plain on the
          other side of the mountain,
to see if anything has changed.
But nothing ever changes.
It is always a soft timeless grey.
And the path upon which a woman flees. Wavering and
          beautiful like a bird
that someone has tried long and unsuccessfully to kill.
And you know that she will always flee just like that.
In front of her, a wall of greyness and behind her, you,
          riddled
with the hollow voices of the locomotives that pass
          through your nights.

The rainy night doesn't live with you.
But you know the cadavers conveyed upon night's glassy
        rope
and you hate them with their own hatred.
They want to take even your misery away.
But you frighten them with their own skulls.

You're safe in the rainy night.
Hidden and alone in a great head of rain
like a chrysalis in the heart of a mountain.

You Are Not

You are not in the voice of the wind, not in the scattered
    mountains,
you are not in the blossoms, and if the birds beckon,
    they do not beckon to you,
you are not in the nakedness of the earth, not in the
    languid odor of the grass,
and if you plant roses to smell of you, they smell
    of themselves,
and if you lay a road, the road will tell its own story,
and if you build a home, if you fill it with precious
    things,
it will one day take you in like a stranger
and the things will talk to themselves in their own
    language,
mocking you.

It's a lie that the spring exists only to quench your thirst,
that the river exists only to bathe you in its cool
    embrace.
It's a lie that things exists only to soothe you
    with tranquil memories,
because one day your whole world will turn against you.

One day the things will change their names,
the stones will hate, the wind will threaten,
the street will frighten, the birds will hammer your brow
with the searing nails of their voices, the river will be
    despair,
your possessions will be your guilt and your accusers.
The world will be in ruins. The world will have no name.

But then you won't care. You'll sit in some forsaken
    corner.

You'll close your eyes and see nothing. Most of all you
         won't see
your own bewilderment in this bewildered and deserted
         world.
So that you won't think that you have to do something,
that you have to walk somewhere on your legs,
which will be as slender as the legs of a black spider.
Only your head will be big. Your head will blossom
white like a magnolia. You will search long in the white
         cave of your mouth
for a name for yourself,
but this time, better than to find a name for going on,
would be to find a name for the end.

from
ROŽENGRUNTAR
1975

Offering

Who walked round himself round his own rotation
Who threw himself was thrown
in the morning between the houses.
Who muttered staggering drunk was twisted
into endless thoughts and labyrinthine places

Erased from the glass.

Light is pure pure is the white cloud
Sliding in the bright depths across silver surfaces
Birds are Flowers are Everyone birds are
gathering in a glass gourd of sound
His halo no longer rotates
around the pointed beams of the world

Old people came and stepped into a circle
singing a song squeezed from their softened heads

And we lick the mouth of the green wolf
we suck the poison fungus from obsolete coins

The Same

It's in another world. The same.
It's the other in the same world. The same.
It's the same in the same world. Other in another.
The same.

He's the same as you. The same hair.
The same hands. The same head.
The same eyes. The same look. The same age.
He's the same.

The same madness. The same love.
The same experience. The same beloved.
Just now thinking the same thoughts
Dancing with the same swinging steps.
In twilight's web, in midnight's snare,
Captured in the same place.
The same.

The same wounds. The same scars.
The same doubts. The same mistakes.
The same hesitations. The same failures.
He is you he senses you.

When you are seen in the cracked light
When you are among people seeing the same
When you sense that you are a shadow of your same self
When he says that he sees you
Oh, what a thought. What a double nothing. Ha.
(He babbles the same words. He twists the same tongue.
The same.)

from
WHITE
1984

Milk

light pours through the cracks
things stir in the gentle morning breeze
the cold stream of nocturnal water dries up
no longer murmurs no longer ripples in the silence
and the mortal cry of the bird
that you heard in the evening
and that glowed in your mind all night
has now faded

you hear a stream of milk squirting from a cow's udder
on to the white floor
and you no longer wonder what happened to
            the screaming in your mind
you open the door and the sun strikes your face
waterfalls of beams and milky light

fearlessly you step outside
and you occupy a body which obeys you
such is your body
as if it would never abandon you
never betray you

White

outside painted light
like a wall stands before our eyes
outside hearing feeling and taste
you are

when we meet our steps become confused
our eyes reel in their sockets
our thoughts, a fist full of dry grass

and we know: the path is spellbound
the path is wrong is lost is the path
the space brightens for an instant
we see it white invisible
you are

soon soon we must leave
the world of sounds colors and tastes
soon only raindrops among sister raindrops
without sound without feeling
like drops we will fall
upon our own white dispossessed bones

soon

Goats

in spring it rolls from the heights
white noise
down down it tumbles
white spring foam from the snowy heights

white goats come
spellbound by the white
running into the white
pure white is this world of whiteness
untrodden untouched
without footsteps without marks

the young goats daringly run
want only to run
playfully the young goats run
on the spotless slope
and when they run to the highest whiteness
the young goats' heads are swept away
into the white they are sown
into a downy white lap
into a white field where only white can survive

in the summer highlanders come
and gather the young goats' heads
tracking them like red flowers in the snow
ripping them from beneath the shrubs
searching for them between the rocks

and stuffing them, aha, into their deep ragged bags

Scorpions

loners
light hurts them
they feed on shards of dusk
they live in worm ridden towers

they are homeless
squeezed between stones
in cracks in crevices
flattened by the weight
rolling over them

sometimes they shoot up up into the silence
up up into the coldness
sometimes their white blood quivers in voiceless song

on the summit of solitude
there under the rainy night
they climb up and let out a silent scream

a distant scream answers from a distant heart
and the screams multiply
in the dismembered depths
deep down under a black sky
they suddenly flash
and silently fade

they live with their stingers
pointed at their own hearts

Mountain

It is a mountain hidden from our eyes.
Sometimes we catch sight of a rock,
sculpted from a different harmony.
It sinks quickly into a pool of water from which
for a single instant the whole world shines.

Sometimes we are roused from sleep
by the sound of singing never heard before.
We behold the shimmering wing
of an unknown bird. It vanishes into
the atmosphere of its own singing.

Sometimes we hear a shrill shrill
murmuring in a wide bare field.
It sounds like wind murmuring through the rocks,
like a waterfall made of white silk
being poured from the sky.

Sometimes between the clouds
we catch sight of a path above the abyss.
It looks like writing across the heights.
We see it only for an instant and we know:
it is the path to the mountain that is not.

The White Weasel

He settled into a home,
and painted paintings on the walls of man.
Ah, paintings, paintings.
And sang songs.
Songs, ah, such songs.

He set things in their place
with a strong unerring hand.
He set them there for many passing years.

But one morning in his garden he spotted,
look there, he spotted a white, white, white
weasel.

Like a streak among the flowers.
It sewed its white thread path
in through the window, out through the roof.
White holes piercing the house.

And he sang no more nor did he paint
and he didn't stop up the white holes
in the fence or in the brittle walls.

But one day one spring day
the man took three hard steps
to ask the weasel.
To ask it what he had always known.

And in that same instant he lay down on his back,
he lay down and looked into the sky.
In and out through his mouth
the weasel streaked.

And it quickly tidied up.
Carrying things out
colors, sounds and tastes
from his soul, thoughts from his songs.

And, aha, looked through one
and, aha, looked though the other
eye.

Into the white the white weasel
disappeared it disappeared.

Yet the home still stands,
half finished, half painted.
But who has finished this home.
But who has painted it.

And sometimes the songs are sung.
And in the middle, silence.
But who has sung this song to the end.

The Executioner

in what hole what cave in what closet what room
eyes half open for no reason
night steals in between dreams and sleep
and who hung this reflection on the cave's wall
and who licked the face of sleep
with a course tongue quickly suddenly coldly
who sliced these eyelids
who cut through hearing so sound could trickle in
who pants with heavy animal breath in this place
who treads with cloven hooves on the bowels of silence

ah I see in the long corridor a stumbling prisoner
ah I see wretchedness in his defeated walk
who sings that quiet song from an anguished throat
but the sentence was already handed down
        and the executioner has risen
who hangs this picture of a broken skull on the wall
but a cold sun is already shining out from the center
        of his body
and the executioner has already seen the name scribbled
        on the paper
has already greased the rope
ah I see him in the empty corridor waiting numb
before a blind window

from
INCANTATIONS
1985

Fire

in a night
as ample and high as the stars
in a silence stretched above peaks
shimmering from their own solitude
a log burns in the fire
rapidly changing form
crackling speaking
a dialogue a trialogue
sparks that spray the darkness
when a solitary voice
swims glows next to me
a voice I feel beneath my ribs
burns

N.Y.

in this empty night flushed with winter light
in these windy streets window window window above
in this thorny silence through which people streak
fast through the air each in his own direction eyes
            turned inward
mutely
skin crawling with goose bumps

he goes through the streets clenched inward
and in a crevice of light his flesh sees a
pale famished shadow holding in its frozen hand
a bright blade that loves his throat

Animals

toward the shining water come the animals
with their taut smooth skin
their legs trembling from thirst
quiet shadows in a white blur
the moon falls toward the water
deep deep clouds pass overhead

the animals drink the shining water
from the passing clouds
the broken moon inhales them through flared nostrils
wind without wind breath without breath
draught without draught

it is night above the land
dew falls from countless eyes

The Girl and the Beast

the house brightens when the girl comes in
her steps on the floor sound softly on the wood
her hand in the water
the water comes to life on her skin
the light from outside falls on her belly
the light from outside doesn't shine off the white glass
it is absorbed not reflected it is drunk drunk by the eye
      of the day
by the girl's smooth skin
in the evening the curious snouts of young animals
press against the door to the house
a lusty star glows
in the straight line across the goat's eye
the scent of the girl's hair spread across her white nape
seeps from the house
the snouts pressed against the cracks sniff
the bitter scent from her underarms
the black line across the goat's eye glows like ignited
      charcoal
when it falls upon the translucent skin of her thighs
which glimmer tautly one against the other
the night grows long long above the house
silence drips long into its depths
the hairy beast pushes into the girl's house
enters it rolls over the bed to the girl
then there are two voices one against the other
the snouts slumber against the cracks
and an eyelid closes over the line in the goat's eye
and when the beast and the girl embrace when the girl
opens her legs and locks the beast between them
the night falls on the other side
growing no more and silence is one with the stars
only the snouts pressed against the cracks streak

through dreams and the goat's sinister line
talks to the stars

the steps of the retreating beast murmur roughly
        through the grass
the house is silent and the girl's soft sleep glows
from her body turned toward the side of morning
the snouts disappear into a cave and the goat bends his
        head
toward his hip and now there are already birds chirping
        as if in a dream
and now the last drop of night slides down from the
        morning star

from the evening tree
an unknown bird with an unknown voice
sings
its singing is half sweet half strange
sweet is white like a turtledove
strange is the sound next to strange
like a dark splendour
when it sings I think of two birds
lifted in one song
together in such a way
that when the double singing
becomes one it falls from height to height
sketched into the swift meandering
of two eternities

a feather falls from the evening sky
a bird's feather into the rift between two worlds
a woman moans in the embrace
of the double voice: one sings
the other whimpers
the bird with the double face
in the evening tree one voice into two
singing eternities

The Last Side of the Mountain

not the one which I climbed
holding my breath beneath the summit
so my sighs wouldn't disturb
the breathing of the mountain
no
it was another mountain
not the one that appears in dreams
always dark always dangerous
its slopes slipping beneath my ascent
I climb with no memory
with no voice and I know its summit
I know that it doesn't exist
it is another

as if it stands between me and the night
only night and the weight of night's gravity
the portal I don't know
never before was it so wide and so quiet
the cold whiteness of two walls opening
I knew that it would wait for me
truth chiselled from dreams
beyond the last step
next to my thin skin
in a swirling voiceless gravity
blossoms the other face of the mountain
with open blade-like petals

The Other Light

the other light fell upon the rocks
lighting up other faces
and the cliffs were changed into another kind of hardness
beneath a quickly fleeing sea
murmuring that it is both under the shore
and high in the air carrying
a different kind of tree a different kind of wind
from behind the mountain to another shore
and the occasional scream is from a hidden world
where it has never been
and the occasional smile of a woman
from her murmuring from her breasts
where his gaze has never touched

perhaps it is another wind that scatters
those two hillocks of dust
the home of a homeless smile
sprinkled into the green murmuring high above him
and the voice that seemed to call to him from an
        overwhelming height
is probably his own voice shrieking
in another place from another time from
his own unknown body

now what that hand is writing
on paper on a knee that knee
is only the impression left by a creature flying
into a wind that has already changed form
and there far away and here close by the mask of her
        smile

Gaya-Quil

helmets set upon swelling heads
march into Gaya's space they stomp
with legs of stone
into the faint odor of skin smelling sweetly
of love's sweat afloat like dust motes
they invade her space they seek out her eyes
pulsing in the corner beneath her hair
frightened animal caught
they seize her open her throw
chains of mail upon her wheezing through
skurvied mouths on her face her hair
Gaya screams once scream after scream
that carries water from this strange helmeted world
to the canal
her scream travels from space to space
where bound Quil holds his blood within white wounds
blood released by the screams like birds
streaking bitterly swiftly through his body

into the cellar they throw
the slender shadows of the two bodies
around them the helmets talk
in the iron language of apathy
from time to time Gaya's red face
glows in the white water of the river
from time to time a woman's knee
in the sunlight shining off the water
a fleeting mirror for the emerald sky
from time to time a hand waves from a branch
from the depths dancing into a fast swirling pool
the body of queen Gaya dances like red mist
above an island of hyacinths
transparently swiftly changing

her face falling into her belly nipples shining piercing
the light from her eyes falling into her mouth
black hyacinths into a rose goblet swallowing swallowing
hair long black hair
carried away by the scream of an unseen bird
escaping beneath a high sky into the water
pulling a scream from a bird which falls from time to
      time

The Herd

morning air on the roof tops
high and low at the same time
the bells that rang in the background of sleep
the muzzles that roared from the bottom of the well
are now departing into the distance
their tattered singing
seeps up through the cracks
like musical instruments buried deep beneath the rocks

and through it all a goat dreams long distorted dreams
his horned head changing form
rearing up here and there and here
he steps before the herd ringing their silver
bells
he is already on the slope of green bilberry shrubs
the herd
of white goats are as white as snowflakes
the metallic song of birds flies up into a rapid
              meandering
then alights in a swirl of mist
the sound of water is transformed into a plait of
shimmering braids

I the Mountain

I am you who is I
your tiny heart in droplets of water
I am built into the walls
when you are me
when you walk on my soil
dressed in grass you walk
on my craggy body
you cling with your knuckles
to my brittle bones
and I lie beneath the sun
shining from a cave into the sky on you
who walks because you are me
when I lie in a great silence
stretched across all four sides of the world
nothing exists except for us
we give form I to you you to me
the secret of the mountain in the mountain
I am the mountain
you the mountain are me
you look at me with my borrowed eyes
that which is motionless and that which walks
are united in the one breath
come evening you sleep
in my body
I the mountain
I am washed in the green milk of twilight

from
DOWN DOWN
1998

This and That

The two walk together
connected, inseparable.
One staggers,
the other supports him.
This one swears,
that one whispers verses
into a sea of his own verses.
This one falls, that one rises
to lift the other up, to comfort him.
Sometimes, only sometimes they are one,
then they shine, then he shines through them.

But they fall apart again.
This one looks into the distance.
That one counts the monsters in his head.
This one hopes fragile hopes.
That one trembles with fear.
They swim in a dark lake
and wave their wartish trunks
in the dark night of his body.

With What Mouth

with what mouth should I speak to you
from what head should I look at you
to what breast should I gather you
with what knife should I cut
your body

into which hollow into which
skin should I place
your soft statue
which words should I whisper to you
in which language the downy
meanings that I place on your
belly

under what roof should I call you
there are no whispers
in this wooden mouth
this tongue is not mine

Golden Hats

gently touch
my lips so they won't remain
swollen with desire

(golden hats smelling sweetly in a quiet sun
the bittersweet smell
of seed mingling
with the scent of a young girl's body)

touch my nipples
with the tip of your tongue
alive impatient
nipples burning
kindled by your lips

(golden hats in throaty depths
dark desire hiding
in pictures where flowery crowns bend down)

only with your fingertips touch
there where you are where I am
so the head will burn red
everything pulsate everything give everything drink
now I press you now I crush you now
I drink you I drink

(golden hats have fallen
crowned heads
the scent of seed mingled with fragrant drops
from a young girl smell sweetly
in the solitary afternoon)

Poetry Ablaze

Fire scans the poems.
Fire adds the punctuation.
A fast burning fire with charred eyes
turns the pages with flaming fingers.

Who will read these verses
written with live embers.
Burnt words. Crumbling syllables.
Distorted letters.

A head impaled on a stake
writes poems from beneath closed eyes.
The head sings us a black poem,
sings mutely from its slit throat.

Golden poems burn, blond hair ablaze.
The illustrious ones burn above the illustrious city.
On scorched wings, with a blackened
warble coming from their beaks.
Roses burn within walled gardens.
Taverns burn, the spires above minarets splinter.
Churches burn.
And one question smoulders in the fire,
what is a poem.

The faces of the clocks burn,
all set ablaze in the same instant.
The past, the future
flicker in the flames of the present.

To the question, what is death,
blood falls
from the mortal wound of a new born child.

Down Down

when I think of the hopes
that were etched in your footprints
I follow them
Footprints that suddenly
sink into the fog and the mud
and the cold wetness

when I expect you and you come
and quietly sit beside me
and ask Is everything is everything alright
In an instant, you ask, in an instant
of carelessness it falls down down
it disappears

I think about how you come with your legs
shining from the treacherous path
how I watch your eyes flickering without reflection
watch the heavy clouds fall
past the sharp edge of the wall
and I hear the needles of the pine trees pierce
the belly of the dark wind

The Crow

In the early morning
he gobbles down starry eyes.
The most delicate part of night's face
cooled on lofty pillows.
He lands on the bed of night
and pecks, pecks.

When he flies, he flies through solitude.
As if through a cave and into another cave,
the cave always going with him, eternally renewed.

When he flies low,
his wings imitate
the voice of the wind, of scythes.
Like wind rushing down from the mountain.
Like scythes slicing the air.

Sometimes he flies with another.
Yet even then his flight
plunges into orbits of solitude.
She follows him
in a quiet distance.
Their feathers don't touch.
They fly each in the space
of their own circle.

He sings different ways.
In three different languages.
Each one meant only for himself.
For his own ear, his own conversation.
He mocks not, bird of hooks.
If he mocks, he mocks only himself,
his own voices, the tangled

speech of his meandering calls.

When he flies low,
his feathers shimmer darkly.
The black defiance of a mysterious realm.

Silences

when you wade naked
into the soft glass of the morning sea
when the clouds are all faces
and between them the highest depths

that place where you gave your word
that country in the sky
transforms, grows, vanishes

there a bird flutters there
under a great mountain
there a star twinkles and doesn't disappear
there bats fly in a staggering chase

in the evening you listen to
the muffled breaths, count them
and you go to a valley where you've never been

breath after breath you count
and you fall
soft as a sigh

The Author

Dane Zajc, born in 1929, is one of the leading voices of modern Slovenian poetry. Zajc was a boy when, during World War II, the Nazis killed members of his family and burned his home and he remained obssesed with the alienation, horror, and anxiety of the contemporary human condition. Having been prevented from pursuing an advanced degree, Zajc worked as a librarian at the children's library in Ljubljana until his recent retirement. A prolific writer of plays, children books, and poems, he is widely recognized as a pillar in the post-war canon of Slovenian letters. His collected works appeared in 1990. He won several awards, including the national Prešeren Prize for lifetime achievement. A former senior Fulbright fellow at Columbia University in New York, Zajc has traveled and given public readings in Latin America and Europe. His poems have been translated into several European languages. This is the first book-length publication of Zajc's verse in English translation.

The Translator

Erica Johnson Debeljak moved from New York to Slovenia in the early nineties. Educated at Columbia and New York Universities, she has translated a number of Slovenian works of literature into English, including several sections in *Afterwards: Slovenian Writing 1945–1995* (edited by Andrew Zawacki; White Pine Press, 2000).

CHRONOLOGY

1929 - Zajc is born on October 26 in Zgornja Javorščica in what was then the Yugoslav Kingdom.

1941–45 - Because of the destruction of the local school, Zajc does not attend school during these years. The occupying forces also burn down his home and two of his brothers die in the partisan resistance struggle.

1948–49 - Zajc begins to publish his poetry in *Youth Journal* *(Mladinska revija)*. These early poems would only be published in book form in 1990, in his *Collected Works* in five volumes.

1951 - Zajc is jailed and expelled from high school. A two-year service in the Yugoslav army follows and hardens his resistance against the communist political system.

1955 - After working for two years for the national postal service, Zajc is employed as a librarian at the Pioneer Youth Library and works there until his retirement in 1989.

1958 - He receives his high school degree following private studies but the pro-regime student organization prevents him from enrolling at the university. Because of barriers posed by the cultural and political bureaucracy, Zajc self-publishes his first collection, *Burnt Grass (Pozgana trava)*.

1961 - His second independent poetry collection, *Tongue of Soil* *(Jezik iz zemlje)* is published.

1962 - Zajc's play, *Children of the River (Otroka reke)* is debuted by the experimental theater *State 57*, which is associated with *Review 57 (Revija 57)*, the magazine Zajc co-founded.

1964 - The cultural journal *Perspectives (Perspektive)* of which

Zajc was the co-editor is banned by the government. Zajc continues to collaborate with dissident publications such as *Word (Beseda)* and *Review 57.*

1968 - Publication of poetry collection *Snake Killers (Ubijavci kač)*.

1975 - Publication of poetry collection *Rožengruntar*.

1979 - Publication of poetry collection *You Saw (Si videl)*.

1981 - Zajc receives the coveted Prešeren Award for his lifetime literary achievements.

1981–82 - Zajc lives and works in New York as a Fulbright visiting writer at Columbia University.

1985 - Publication of poetry collection *Incantations (Zarotitve)*.

1991–1995 - President of the Slovenian Writers Association.

1993 - Becomes a member of Slovenian Academy of Arts and Sciences.

1998 - Publication of poetry collection *Down Down (Dol dol)* for which Zajc wins the national Jenko Poetry Award.

In addition to the books listed above, Dane Zajc has written many theatrical plays, children's poetry collections and essays. His work has been published in several anthologies and has appeared in book form in Serbian, Macedonian, German, Swedish and French translations. Besides the above mentioned awards, Zajc has received many literary prizes in the former Yugoslavia and Slovenia.

The Terra Incognita Series
Writing from Central Europe

Series Editor: Aleš Debeljak

Volume 8
Barren Harvest
Selected Poems of Dane Zajc
Translated by Erica Johnson Debeljak
112 pages $14.00

Volume 7
Plum Brandy: Croatian Journeys
Essays by Josip Novakovich
182 pages $16.00

Volume 6
Perched on Nothing's Branch
Poems by Attila Jozsef
Edited by Peter Hargitai
80 pages $14.00

Volume 5
The City and the Child
Poems by Aleš Debeljak
96 pages $14.00

Volume 4
Afterwards: Slovenian Writing 1945-1995
Edited by Andrew Zawacki
250 pages $17.00

Volume 3
Heart of Darkness
Poems by Ferida Duraković
112 pages $14.00